FORWARD/COMMENTARY

The National Institute of Standards and Technology (NIST) is a measurement standards laboratory, and a non-regulatory agency of the United States Department of Commerce. Its mission is to promote innovation and industrial competitiveness. Founded in 1901, as the National Bureau of Standards, NIST was formed with the mandate to provide standard weights and measures, and to serve as the national physical laboratory for the United States. With a world-class measurement and testing laboratory encompassing a wide range of areas of computer science, mathematics, statistics, and systems engineering, NIST's cybersecurity program supports its overall mission to promote U.S. innovation and industrial competitiveness by advancing measurement science, standards, and related technology through research and development in ways that enhance economic security and improve our quality of life.

The need for cybersecurity standards and best practices that address interoperability, usability and privacy has been shown to be critical for the nation. NIST's cybersecurity programs seek to enable greater development and application of practical, innovative security technologies and methodologies that enhance the country's ability to address current and future computer and information security challenges.

The cybersecurity publications produced by NIST cover a wide range of cybersecurity concepts that are carefully designed to work together to produce a holistic approach to cybersecurity primarily for government agencies and constitute the best practices used by industry. This holistic strategy to cybersecurity covers the gamut of security subjects from development of secure encryption standards for communication and storage of information while at rest to how best to recover from a cyber-attack.

Why buy a book you can download for free?   We print this so you don't have to.

Some are available only in electronic media. Some online docs are missing pages or barely legible.

We at 4th Watch Publishing are former government employees, so we know how government employees actually use the standards. When a new standard is released, an engineer prints it out, punches holes and puts it in a 3-ring binder. While this is not a big deal for a 5 or 10-page document, many NIST documents are over 100 pages and printing a large document is a time-consuming effort. So, an engineer that's paid $75 an hour is spending hours simply printing out the tools needed to do the job. That's time that could be better spent doing engineering. We publish these documents so engineers can focus on what they were hired to do – engineering. It's much more cost-effective to just order the latest version from Amazon.com

If there is a standard you would like published, let us know. Our web site is usgovpub.com

Many of our titles are available as eBooks for Kindle, iPad, Nook, remarkable, BOOX, and Sony eReaders. Buy the paperback from Amazon and get Kindle eBook FREE using MATCHBOOK. Go to https://usgovpub.com to learn more.

Why buy an eBook when you can access data on a website for free? HYPERLINKS

Yes, many books are available as a PDF, but not all PDFs are bookmarked? Do you really want to search a 6,500-page PDF document manually? Load our copy onto your Kindle, PC, iPad, Android Tablet, Nook, or iPhone (download the FREE kindle App from the APP Store) and you have an easily searchable copy. Most devices will allow you to easily navigate an ePub to any Chapter. Note that there is a distinction between a Table of Contents and "Page Navigation". Page Navigation refers to a different sort of Table of Contents. Not one appearing as a page in the book, but one that shows up on the device itself when the reader accesses the navigation feature. Readers can click on a navigation link to jump to a Chapter or Subchapter. Once there, most devices allow you to "pinch and zoom" in or out to easily read the text. (Unfortunately, downloading the free sample file at Amazon.com does not include this feature. You have to buy a copy to get that functionality, but as inexpensive as eBooks are, it's worth it.) Kindle allows you to do word search and Page Flip (temporary place holder takes you back when you want to go back and check something). Visit **USGOVPUB.COM** to learn more.

NIST Special Publication 800-163
Revision 1

Vetting the Security of
Mobile Applications

Michael Ogata
Josh Franklin
Jeffrey Voas
Vincent Sritapan
Stephen Quirolgico

C O M P U T E R   S E C U R I T Y

National Institute of
Standards and Technology
U.S. Department of Commerce

NIST Special Publication 800-163
Revision 1

Vetting the Security of Mobile Applications

Michael Ogata
Software and Systems Division
Information Technology Laboratory

Josh Franklin*
Applied Cybersecurity Division
Information Technology Laboratory

Jeffrey Voas
Computer Security Division
Information Technology Laboratory

Vincent Sritapan
Office of Science and Technology
U.S. Department of Homeland Security

Stephen Quirolgico
Office of the Chief Information Officer
U.S. Department of Homeland Security

*Former employee; all work for this
publication was done while at NIST

This publication is available free of charge from:
https://doi.org/10.6028/NIST.SP.800-163r1

April 2019

U.S. Department of Commerce
Wilbur L. Ross, Jr., Secretary

National Institute of Standards and Technology
Walter Copan, NIST Director and Under Secretary of Commerce for Standards and Technology

Authority

This publication has been developed by NIST in accordance with its statutory responsibilities under the Federal Information Security Modernization Act (FISMA) of 2014, 44 U.S.C. § 3551 *et seq.*, Public Law (P.L.) 113-283. NIST is responsible for developing information security standards and guidelines, including minimum requirements for federal information systems, but such standards and guidelines shall not apply to national security systems without the express approval of appropriate federal officials exercising policy authority over such systems. This guideline is consistent with the requirements of the Office of Management and Budget (OMB) Circular A-130.

Nothing in this publication should be taken to contradict the standards and guidelines made mandatory and binding on federal agencies by the Secretary of Commerce under statutory authority. Nor should these guidelines be interpreted as altering or superseding the existing authorities of the Secretary of Commerce, Director of the OMB, or any other federal official. This publication may be used by nongovernmental organizations on a voluntary basis and is not subject to copyright in the United States. Attribution would, however, be appreciated by NIST.

National Institute of Standards and Technology Special Publication 800-163 Revision 1
Natl. Inst. Stand. Technol. Spec. Publ. 800-163 Rev. 1, 55 pages (April 2019)
CODEN: NSPUE2

This publication is available free of charge from:
https://doi.org/10.6028/NIST.SP.800-163r1

Certain commercial entities, equipment, or materials may be identified in this document in order to describe an experimental procedure or concept adequately. Such identification is not intended to imply recommendation or endorsement by NIST, nor is it intended to imply that the entities, materials, or equipment are necessarily the best available for the purpose.

There may be references in this publication to other publications currently under development by NIST in accordance with its assigned statutory responsibilities. The information in this publication, including concepts and methodologies, may be used by federal agencies even before the completion of such companion publications. Thus, until each publication is completed, current requirements, guidelines, and procedures, where they exist, remain operative. For planning and transition purposes, federal agencies may wish to closely follow the development of these new publications by NIST.

Organizations are encouraged to review all draft publications during public comment periods and provide feedback to NIST. Many NIST cybersecurity publications, other than the ones noted above, are available at https://csrc.nist.gov/publications.

Comments on this publication may be submitted to:

National Institute of Standards and Technology
Attn: Computer Security Division, Information Technology Laboratory
100 Bureau Drive (Mail Stop 8930) Gaithersburg, MD 20899-8930
Email: nist800-163@nist.gov

All comments are subject to release under the Freedom of Information Act (FOIA).

Reports on Computer Systems Technology

The Information Technology Laboratory (ITL) at the National Institute of Standards and Technology (NIST) promotes the U.S. economy and public welfare by providing technical leadership for the Nation's measurement and standards infrastructure. ITL develops tests, test methods, reference data, proof of concept implementations, and technical analyses to advance the development and productive use of information technology. ITL's responsibilities include the development of management, administrative, technical, and physical standards and guidelines for the cost-effective security and privacy of other than national security-related information in federal information systems. The Special Publication 800-series reports on ITL's research, guidelines, and outreach efforts in information system security, and its collaborative activities with industry, government, and academic organizations.

Abstract

Mobile applications are an integral part of our everyday personal and professional lives. As both public and private organizations rely more on mobile applications, ensuring that they are reasonably free from vulnerabilities and defects becomes paramount. This paper outlines and details a mobile application vetting process. This process can be used to ensure that mobile applications conform to an organization's security requirements and are reasonably free from vulnerabilities.

Keywords

app vetting; app vetting system; malware; mobile applications; mobile security; NIAP; security requirements; software assurance; software vulnerabilities; software testing.

Trademark Information

Table of Contents

List of Appendices

List of Figures

List of Tables

1   Introduction

Mobile applications (or *apps*) have had a transformative effect on organizations. Through ever-increasing functionality, ubiquitous connectivity and faster access to mission-critical information, mobile apps continue to provide unprecedented support for facilitating organizational objectives. Despite their utility, these apps can pose serious security risks to an organization and its users due to vulnerabilities that may exist within their software [1].Such vulnerabilities may be exploited to steal information, control a user's device, deplete hardware resources, or result in unexpected app or device behavior.

App vulnerabilities are caused by several factors including design flaws and programming errors, which may have been inserted intentionally or inadvertently. In the app marketplace, apps containing vulnerabilities are prevalent due in part to the submission of apps by developers who may trade security for functionality in order to reduce cost and time to market.

The commercial app stores provided by mobile operating system vendors (Android, iOS) review the apps for issues such as malware, objectionable content, collecting user information without notice, performance impact (e.g., battery), etc. prior to allowing them to be hosted in their app market. The level and type of reviews conducted are opaque to consumers and the federal government. Furthermore, these app markets serve a global customer base that numbers in the billions and their reviews of apps are consumer- and brand-focused. Enterprise organizations—federal agencies, regulated industries, other non-governmental organizations—that plan to use consumer apps for their business will need to make risk-based decisions for app acquisition based on their own security, privacy and policy requirements and risk tolerance.

The level of risk related to vulnerabilities varies depending on several factors including the data accessible to an app. For example, apps that access data such as precise and continuous geolocation information, personal health metrics or personally identifiable information (PII) may be considered to be of higher risk than those that do not access sensitive data. In addition, apps that depend on wireless network technologies (e.g., Wi-Fi, cellular, Bluetooth) for data transmission may also be of high risk since these technologies also can be used as vectors for remote exploits. Even apps considered low risk, however, can have significant impact if exploited. For example, public safety apps that fail due to a vulnerability exploit could potentially result in the loss of life.

To mitigate potential security risks associated with mobile apps, organizations should employ a software assurance process that ensures a level of confidence that software is free from vulnerabilities, either intentionally designed into the software or accidentally inserted at any time during its life cycle, and that the software functions in the intended manner [2]. In this document, we define a software assurance process for mobile applications. We refer to this process as an *app vetting process*.

---

[1] A vulnerability is defined as one or more weaknesses that can be accidentally triggered or intentionally exploited and result in a
    violation of desired system properties [1]

1.1   Purpose

This document defines an app vetting process and provides guidance on (1) planning and implementing an app vetting process, (2) developing security requirements for mobile apps, (3) identifying appropriate tools for testing mobile apps and (4) determining if a mobile app is acceptable for deployment on an organization's mobile devices. An overview of techniques commonly used by software assurance professionals is provided, including methods of testing for discrete software vulnerabilities and misconfigurations related to mobile app software.

1.2   Scope

Software assurance activities for a mobile application may occur in one or more phases of the mobile application lifecycle: (1) during the development of the app by its developer (i.e., the app development phase), (2) after receiving a developed app but prior to its deployment by the end-user organization (i.e., the app acquisition phase) or (3) during deployment of the app by the end-user organization (i.e., the app deployment phase). These three phases of the mobile application lifecycle are shown in Figure 1.

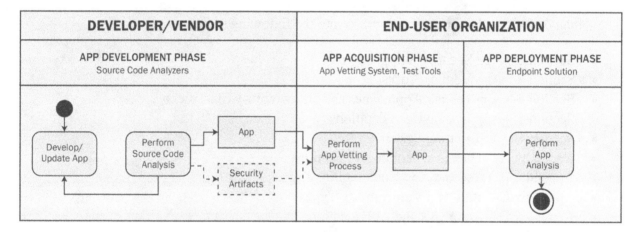

Figure 1 - Software assurance during mobile application lifecycle.

In this document, we focus primarily on the software assurance activities of the app vetting process, which we define as part of the app acquisition phase of the mobile application lifecycle. Thus, software assurance activities performed during the app's development phase (e.g., by source code analyzers) or during the app's deployment phase (e.g., by endpoint solutions) are considered out of scope for this document.

In addition, this document does not address the use of Enterprise Mobility Management (EMM), mobile app management or mobile threat defense systems, although integrations with these systems are briefly examined. Further, this document does not discuss vetting the security of Internet of Things (IoT) apps or address the security of underlying mobile platforms and operating systems. These subjects are addressed in other publications [3]–[5]. Finally, discussion surrounding the security of web services and cloud infrastructures used to support backend processing of apps is also out of scope for this document.

Finally, it should be noted that mobile apps, and the devices they run on, communicate using a variety of network infrastructures: Wi-Fi, cellular networks, Bluetooth, etc. These networks represent possible failure points for the security of an app. A deep evaluation of each of these network infrastructures is out of scope for this document.

1.3   Intended Audience

This document is intended for public- and private-sector organizations that seek to improve the software assurance of mobile apps deployed on their mobile devices. More specifically, this document is intended for those who are:

- Responsible for establishing an organization's mobile device security posture,
- Responsible for the management and security of mobile devices within an organization,
- Responsible for determining which apps are used within an organization, and
- Interested in understanding what types of assurances the app vetting process provides.

1.4   Document Structure

The remainder of this document is organized into the following sections:

- Section 2—App Security Requirements
- Section 3—App Vetting Process
- Section 4—App Testing Approaches and Vulnerability Classifiers
- Section 5—App Vetting Considerations
- Section 6—App Vetting Systems
- Appendix A—Threats to Mobile Applications
- Appendix B—Android App Vulnerability Types
- Appendix C— iOS App Vulnerability Types
- Appendix D—Acronyms and Abbreviations
- Appendix E—Glossary
- Appendix F—References

1.5   Document Conventions

Applications written specifically for a mobile platform are referred to as "apps" throughout this special publication.

2   App Security Requirements

Before vetting a mobile app for security, an organization must define the security requirements that an app must meet in order to be approved for use by the organization. In this document, we define two types of app security requirements that organizations should develop: *general* and *organization-specific*.

2.1   General Requirements

General app security requirements define the software and behavioral characteristics of an app that should or should not be present in order to ensure the security of the app. These requirements are considered "general" since they can be applied across all mobile applications and tailored to meet the security needs and risk tolerance of an organization. General app security requirements may be derived from a number of available standards, best practices, and resources including those specified by NIAP, OWASP, MITRE and NIST[2].

2.1.1   National Information Assurance Partnership (NIAP)

The NIAP Protection Profiles (PPs) specify an implementation-independent set of security requirements for a category of information technology (IT) products that meet specific federal customer needs. Specifically, the NIAP PPs are intended for use in certifying products for use in national security systems to meet a defined set of security requirements. NIAP PP certified products are also used by federal organizations in non-national security systems. The NIAP PPs define in detail the security objectives, requirements and assurance activities that must be met for a product evaluation to be considered International Organization for Standardization (ISO)/ International Electrotechnical Commission (IEC) 15408 certified [6]. While many mobile apps fall outside the defined scope for requiring ISO/IEC 15408 certification, security analysis of these apps is still useful. For these apps, the NIAP recommends a set of activities and evaluations defined in Requirements for Vetting Mobile Apps from the Protection Profile for Application Software [7]. The requirements defined in this document are divided into two broad categories:

1) Functional Requirements—Declarations concerning the required existence or absence of particular software behavior or attributes.
2) Assurance Requirements—Declarations concerning actions the evaluator must take or stipulations that must be true for vetting to successfully execute.

Table 1 summarizes the NIAP functional requirements[3].

---

[2] Additional threats and vulnerabilities can be found in Appendices A, B, and C.

[3] For brevity, many, but not all the functional requirements are listed in Table 1. Some are high-level descriptions of multiple related controls. See NIAP Protection Profile for the full list [7].

Table 1 - NIAP Functional Requirements.

Functional Requirements
Access to Platform Resources
Anti-Exploitation Capabilities
Cryptographic Key Functionality
Cryptographic Operations
Encryption of Sensitive Application Data
Hyper Text Transfer Protocol Secure (HTTPS)
Integrity for Installation and Update
Network Communications
Protection of Data in Transit
Random Bit Generation
Secure by Default Configuration
Software Identification and Versions
Specification of Management Functions
Storage of Credentials
Supported Configuration Mechanism
Transport Layer Security Operations
Use of Supported Services and Application Programming Interfaces
Use of Third-Party Libraries
User Consent for Transmission of Personally Identifiable Information
X.509 Functionality

The Assurance Requirement found in the protection profile can be summarized as follows:

- The application shall be labeled with a unique reference.
- The evaluator shall test a subset of the Target of Evaluation (TOE) security functions (TSF) to confirm that the TSF operates as specified.
- The application shall be suitable for testing (free from obfuscation[4])
- The evaluator shall perform a search of public domain sources to identify potential vulnerabilities in the TOE.

2.1.2 OWASP Mobile Risks, Controls and App Testing Guidance

The Open Web Application Security Project (OWASP) maintains multiple useful resources concerning mobile app testing and security. Their Mobile Application Security Verification Standard (MASVS) [8] is a detailed model for mobile app security that can be used to provide baseline security requirements for an organization. Like the NIAP PP, the MASVS defines a set

---

[4] It should be noted that code obfuscation has legitimate uses in industry as a method to attempt to safeguard apps and intellectual property. In cases where obfuscated apps need to be analyzed, organizations could leverage businesses relationships with app developers to circumvent these precautions for the duration of the analysis.

of declarations concerning the structure and behavior of an app. However, the MASVS also defines three verification levels:

- Standard Security (Level 1)
- Defense in Depth (Level 2)
- Resilience against Reverse Engineering and Threats (Level 3).

Each level's control lists are divided into the categories listed below, with the object described for each control depending on the desired verification level:

- Architecture, Design, and Threat Modeling Requirements

- Data Storage and Privacy Requirements

- Cryptography Requirements

- Authentication and Session Management Requirements

- Network Communication Requirements

- Platform Integration Requirements

- Code Quality and Build-Setting Requirements

- Resilience Requirements

The OWASP Mobile Security Testing Guide (MSTG) [9] is a manual for testing the security of mobile apps. It describes the technical processes for verifying the requirements listed in the MASVS.

2.1.3   MITRE App Evaluation Criteria

In 2016, the MITRE Corporation (MITRE) performed an analysis of the effectiveness of mobile app security vetting solutions for helping enterprises automate portions of their vetting process. To perform the analysis, MITRE developed solution criteria based on NIAP's Protection Profile for Application Software as well as additional criteria to address broader app vetting solution capabilities, threats against the app vetting solution itself, and other common mobile app vulnerabilities and malicious behaviors.

Using its criteria, MITRE developed or obtained multiple vulnerable and malicious-appearing apps for use in assessing mobile app vetting solutions. MITRE used the apps to test the capabilities of mobile app vetting solutions.

MITRE published a technical report [10] describing their methodology, evaluation criteria, test applications and overall results from analyzing then-available solutions. The report and test applications are available on MITRE's GitHub site[5].

2.1.4   NIST SP 800-53

NIST Special Publication 800-53 [5] provides an extensive catalog of security and privacy controls designed for federal information systems. In addition, the document defines a process for selecting controls to defend IT systems, individuals and other organizational assets from a variety of threats, such as hostile cyber-attacks, natural disasters, structural failures and human errors. The controls can be customized to an organization-specific process to manage information security and privacy risk. The controls can support a diverse set of security and privacy requirements across an organization's required policies, standards, and/or business needs. A set of three security control baseline are provided based on high, medium and low impact. Going further, the publication also describes how to develop specialized sets of controls, also known as control overlays, that can be tailored for unique, or specific types of missions/business functions and technologies. The NIST 800-53 security controls address privacy and security from a functionality perspective (the strength of security functions and mechanisms provided) and an assurance perspective (the measures of confidence in the implemented security capability). Addressing both security functionality and security assurance ensures that information technology products and the information systems built from those products using sound systems and security engineering principles are sufficiently trustworthy.

2.2   Organization-Specific Requirements

Organization-specific security requirements define the policies, regulations and guidance that an organization must follow to ensure the security posture of the organization. Examples include banning social media apps from installation on the organization's mobile devices and restricting installation of apps developed by specific vendors.

To help develop organization-specific security requirements, it is helpful to identify non-vulnerability-related factors that can impact the security posture of mobile apps. Such factors can be derived by considering the criteria as shown in Table 2.

Table 2 - Organization-specific security criteria.

Criterion	Description
Policies	The security, privacy and acceptable use policies; social media guidelines; and regulations applicable to the organization.
Provenance	Identity of the developer, developer's organization, developer's reputation, consumer reviews, etc.
	The level of importance of the app relative to the organization's business.
	The app's intended set of users from the organization.
Target Hardware	The intended hardware platform on which the app will be deployed.

---

[5] https://github.com/mitre/vulnerable-mobile-apps

Target Operating Platform	The operating system, operating system version/Software Development Kit (SDK), and configuration on which the app will be deployed.		
Target Environment	The intended operational environment of the app (e.g., general public use vs. sensitive military environment).		
Digital Signature	Digital signatures applied to the app binaries, libraries, or packages.		
App Documentation	User Guide	When available, the app's user guide assists testing by specifying the expected functionality and expected behaviors. This is simply a statement from the developer describing what they claim their app does and how it does it.	
	Test Plans	Reviewing the developer's test plans may help focus app vetting by identifying any areas that have not been tested or were tested inadequately. A developer could opt to submit a test oracle in certain situations to demonstrate its internal test effort.	
	Test Results	Code review results and other testing results will indicate which security standards were followed. For example, if an app threat model was created, this standard should be submitted. It will list weaknesses that were identified and should have been addressed during app design and coding.	
	Service-Level Agreement	If an app was developed for an organization by a third-party, a Service-Level Agreement (SLA) may have been included as part of the vendor contract. This contract should require the app to be compatible with the organization's security policy.	

Some information can be gleaned from app documentation in certain cases, but even if documentation does exist it might lack technical clarity and/or use jargon specific to the circle of users who would normally purchase the app. Since the documentation for different apps will be structured in different ways, it may also be time-consuming to find this information for evaluation. Therefore, a standardized questionnaire might be appropriate for determining the software's purpose and assessing an app developer's efforts to address security weaknesses. Such questionnaires aim to identify software quality issues and security weaknesses by helping developers address questions from end-users/adopters about their software development processes. For example, developers can use the Department of Homeland Security (DHS) Custom Software Questionnaire [11] to answer questions such as *"Does your software validate inputs from untrusted resources?"* and *"What threat assumptions were made when designing protections for your software?"* Another useful question, not included in the DHS questionnaire, is: *"Does your app access a network application programming interface (API)?"* Note that such questionnaires can be used only in certain circumstances such as when source code is available and when developers can answer questions.

Known flaws in app design and coding may be reported in publicly accessible vulnerability databases such as the U.S. National Vulnerability Database (NVD).[6] Before conducting the full vetting process for a publicly available app, analysts should check one or more vulnerability databases to determine if there are known flaws in the corresponding version of the app. If one or more serious flaws already have been discovered, this finding alone might be sufficient grounds to reject the version of the app for organizational use, thus allowing the rest of the vetting

---

[6] Vulnerability databases generally reference vulnerabilities by their Common Vulnerabilities and Exposures (CVE) identifier. For more information about CVE, see [12].

process to be skipped. However, in most cases such flaws will not be known, and the full vetting process will be needed. This necessity is because there are many forms of vulnerabilities other than known flaws in app design and coding. Identifying these weaknesses necessitates first defining the app security requirements, so that deviations from these requirements can be flagged as weaknesses.

In some cases, an organization will have no defined organization-specific requirements. As a result, analysts will evaluate the security posture of the app based solely on reports and risk assessments from test tools.

Note that the satisfaction or violation of an organization-specific requirement is not based on the presence or absence of a software vulnerability and thus cannot typically be determined by test tools. Instead, the satisfaction or violation of organization-specific requirements must be determined manually by an analyst.

2.3   Risk Management and Risk Tolerance

The NIST Risk Management Framework (RMF) represents a joint effort spearheaded by NIST, the Department of Defense (DoD), and the Committee on National Security Systems (CNSS). The RMF describes a process through which an organization establishes, maintains and communicates a strategy to manage organization *risk* in relation to an *information system* [13]. The RMF is a seven-step process consisting of the following steps:

- **Step 0: Prepare** – identifying key individuals and their assigned roles within the organization, as well as the identification, organization, and prioritization of required resources
- **Step 1: Categorize** – identifying the security requirements associated with a system by classifying the system according to legislation, policies, directives, regulations, standards, and organizational mission/business/operational requirements
- **Step 2: Select** – determining the baseline set of security controls that match the organization's risk tolerance
- **Step 3: Implement** – implementing and documentation of selected controls
- **Step 4: Assess** – examining the implementation of the security controls with respect to the organization's requirements
- **Step 5: Authorize** – enabling the system to be used within the organization
- **Step 6: Monitor** – ongoing and/or reoccurring reassessment of the selected security controls

Figure 2 describes the relationship between the steps of the RMF, as well as showing appropriate supporting documentation for each step:

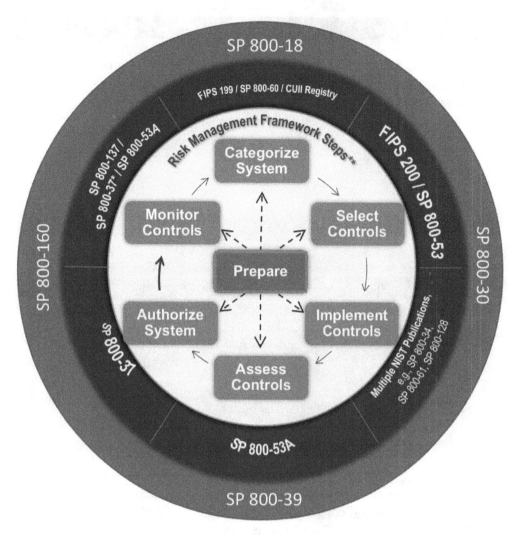

Figure 2 - Risk Management Framework

A key activity in Step 0 involves identifying an organization's risk tolerance [14]. Risk tolerance is the level of risk, or degree of uncertainty, that is acceptable to an organization [15]. A defined risk tolerance level identifies the degree to which an organization should be protected against confidentiality, integrity or availability compromise.

Risk tolerance should take into account the following factors:

- Compliance with security regulations, recommendations and best practices;
- Privacy risks;
- Security threats;
- Data and asset value;
- Industry and competitive pressure; and
- Management preferences.

3   App Vetting Process

An app vetting process is a sequence of activities performed by an organization to determine if a mobile app conforms to the organization's app security requirements[7]. If an app is found to conform to the organization's app security requirements, the app is typically accepted for deployment on the organization's devices. An overview of the app vetting process is shown in Figure 3.

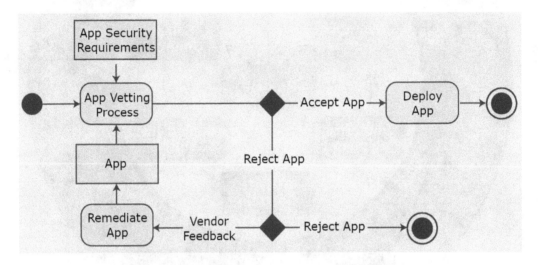

Figure 3 - App vetting process overview.

Although app vetting processes may vary among organizations, each instance of the process should be repeatable, efficient and consistent. The process should also limit errors to the extent possible (e.g., false-positive results). Typically, an app vetting process is performed manually or by an app vetting system that manages and automates all or part of the app vetting activities [16]. As part of an app vetting system, one or more test tools may be used to analyze an app for the existence of software vulnerabilities or malicious behavior consistent with malware.

As shown in Figure 1, organizations perform an app vetting process during the app acquisition phase of a mobile application lifecycle; that is, when the app is received by the organization but prior to the app's deployment on the organization's devices. The rationale for this approach stems from the fact that while developers may perform their own software assurance processes on an app, there is no guarantee the app will conform to an organization's security requirements. Furthermore, because testing of the app by the developer occurs outside the vetting process, an organization must trust the work of these previously-performed assurance activities. Organizations should not assume an app has been fully vetted or conforms to their security requirements simply because it is available through an official app store.

---

[7] An app vetting process also can be used to assess other issues including reliability, performance and accessibility, but is primarily intended to assess security-related issues.

It should be noted, when organizations have a close relationship with the app developer, the core loop of app vetting→rejection→vendor feedback→app vetting shown in Figure 3 can be accelerated if organizations are tightly embedded in an app developer's testing infrastructure. That is, organizations can leverage modern agile software development models [17] to better meet their security requirements.

Performing an app vetting process prior to deployment on a mobile device affords certain benefits including rigorous and comprehensive analysis that can leverage scalable computational resources. Furthermore, since testing occurs before deployment, the vetting process is not limited by timing constraints for remediating discovered threats. However, while this document focuses on the vetting of mobile apps during the organization's app acquisition phase, NIST recommends organizations also perform security analysis during the deployment phase using, for example, an endpoint solution on a mobile device.

An app vetting process comprises four sub-processes: app intake, app testing, app approval/rejection, and results submission processes. These processes are shown in Figure 4.

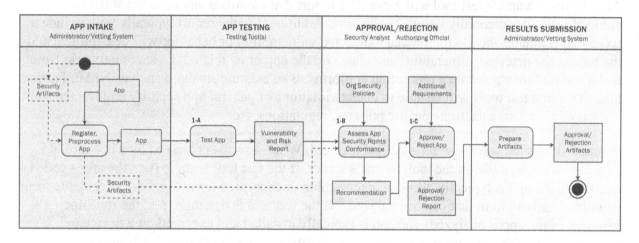

Figure 4 - Four sub-processes of an app vetting process.

3.1 App Intake

The app intake process begins when an app is received for analysis. This process is typically performed manually by an organization administrator or automatically by an app vetting system. The app intake process has two primary inputs: the app under consideration (required) and additional testing artifacts such as reports from previous app vetting results (optional).

After receiving an app, the app may be registered by recording information about the app including developer information, time and data of submission, and any other relevant information needed for the app vetting process. After registration, an app may also be preprocessed. Preprocessing typically involves decoding or decompiling the app to extract required meta-data (e.g., app name, version number) and to confirm that the app can be properly decoded or decompiled since test tools may need to perform this operation prior to performing their analyses.

In addition to the app itself, the app developer may optionally provide software assurance artifacts including previous security analysis reports. It should be noted that organizations accepting these artifacts must accept the validity and integrity of app quality statements made by the artifacts at the word of the app developer.

3.2   App Testing

The app testing process begins after an app has been registered and preprocessed and is forwarded to one or more test tools. A test tool is a software tool or service that tests an app for the presence of software vulnerabilities[8]. Such testing will involve the use of different analysis methodologies (e.g., static analysis) and may be performed manually or automatically. Note that the tests performed by a test tool may identify software vulnerabilities that are common across different apps and will often satisfy general app security requirements (such as those specified by NIAP).

After testing an app, a test tool will generate a report that identifies any detected software vulnerabilities or potentially harmful behaviors. Additionally, the report typically will include a score that estimates the likelihood that a detected vulnerability or behavior will be exploited and the impact the detected vulnerability may have on the app or its related device or network. Note that a test tool may generate a report that conforms to an existing standard such as NIAP. Further note that some test tools will be able to detect violations of general app security requirements but not violations of organization-specific policies, regulations, etc.

Figure 5 shows the workflow for a typical test tool. When an app is received by a test tool, it is typically saved as a file on the tool vendor's server. If the test tool is static (i.e., the app's code is analyzed), the app is typically decoded, decompiled or decrypted from its binary executable form to an intermediate form that can be analyzed.[9] If the test tool is dynamic (i.e., the run-time behavior of the app is analyzed), the app is typically installed and executed on a device or emulator where the behavior of the app can be analyzed. After the tool analyzes the app, it generates a vulnerability report and risk assessment and submits this report to the app vetting system.

---

[8] Section 4 describes techniques and approaches used by app vetting tools.

[9] Typically, decoded or decompiled code does not result in source code, but rather an intermediate code that can be analyzed.

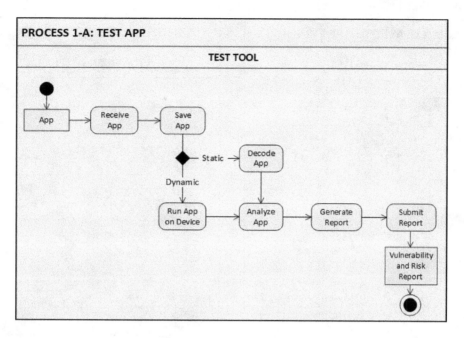

Figure 5 - Test tool workflow.

3.3   App Approval/Rejection

The app approval/rejection process begins after a vulnerability and risk report is generated by a test tool and made available to one or more security analysts. A security analyst (or *analyst*) inspects vulnerability reports and risk assessments from one or more test tools to ensure that an app meets all general app security requirements. An analyst will also evaluate organization-specific app security requirements to determine if an app violates any security policies or regulations. After evaluating all general and organization-specific app security requirements, an analyst will collate this information into a report that specifies a recommendation for approving or rejecting the app for deployment on the organization's mobile devices.

The recommendation report from an analyst is then made available to an authorizing official, who is a senior official of the organization responsible for determining which apps will be deployed on the organization's mobile devices. An authorizing official decides the approval or rejection of an app using the recommendations provided by the analysts and considers other organization-specific (non-security-related) criteria including cost, need, etc. The analyst may add potential mitigating controls for some findings such as the use of a per-app Virtual Private Network (VPN) to protect data in transit. When making the app determination, the authorizing official considers these mitigations as well the sensitivity of data generated or accessed by the app, the type of users and how the app will be used, who owns and manages the device and whether the app will access back-end systems or data (see Step 1of the Risk Management Framework [13]). These analyst reports describe the app's security posture as well as possibly other non-security-related requirements. The organization's official approval or rejection is specified in a final approval/rejection report. Figure 6 shows the app approval/rejection process.

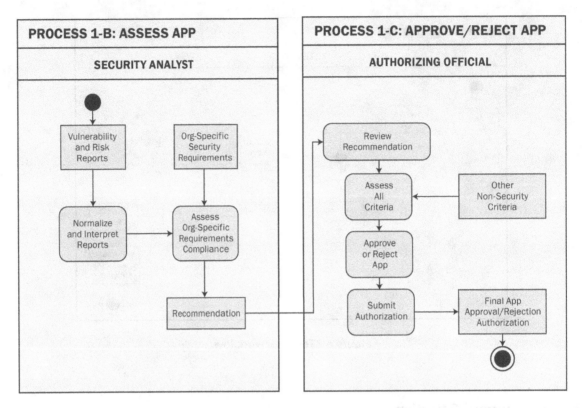

Figure 6 - App approval/rejection process.

3.4   Results Submission

The results submission process begins after the final app approval/rejection report is finalized by the authorizing official and artifacts are prepared for submission to the requesting source. These artifacts may include the final approval/rejection report, test tool reports and possibly a digitally signed version of the app that indicates the app has completed the app vetting process. The use of a digital signature provides source authentication and integrity protection, attesting that the version of the analyzed app is the same as the version that was initially submitted and was not deliberately modified.

3.5   App Re-Vetting

The threat landscape for mobile apps is a constantly moving target. As time progresses, new vulnerabilities are discovered. Likewise, the tools used to identify them attempt to keep pace. As such, vulnerabilities can be discovered in an app at any point of an app's lifecycle, even post deployment. Furthermore, the current paradigm of mobile app development allows for apps to receive multiple updates and patches that add functionality, provide bug fixes, and patch vulnerabilities. From the perspective of a security analyst, these updates can force the evaluation of updated apps to be treated as wholly new pieces of software. Depending on the risk tolerance of an organization, this can make the re-vetting of mobile apps critical for certain apps. Organizations will need to establish protocols for what conditions trigger app re-vetting. A complete analysis of these triggers is out of scope for this document. However, organizations should consider the following when establishing their re-vetting policies:

- Depending on the risk tolerance of an organization, applications that are not receiving regular updates can be re-vetting periodically (e.g. quarterly, biannually, annually) to benefit from improved analysis tools and techniques.
- Organizations can leverage business relationships with app developers who purpose build applications for their use to understand the degree to which app updates may affect an app's risk profile.
- If allowed/enforced by organization policy, apps originating from commercial app stores can receive updates automatically. This can occur either by allowing devices to pull app updates directly from their respective app store or by having Mobile Application Management (MAM)[10] software push updated apps to enrolled devices. These actions can dramatically alter the risk profile of an organization at scale.

Ideally, an organization would be able to track and analyze all apps after an update prior to allowing installation; however, this is resource intensive and introduces delay for users. Some app security vendors provide 'continuous mobile app vetting' of an organization's managed apps through automated tracking of installed apps and security analysis of updates. While this practice doesn't stop app updates that are pushed to a device, it does reduce the window of exposure for a potentially vulnerable updated app.

---

[10] See Section 5.2 for an overview of MAM technology.

4   App Testing and Vulnerability Classifiers

During the app testing process, test tools are used to test for the existence of app vulnerabilities and malicious behavior. Often, such tools are based on standards such as NIAP and thus, may be used to used determine the satisfaction of general app security requirements. This section covers some of the strategies and approaches used by test tools and services to analyze mobile apps for vulnerabilities. It also describes various classifiers and quantifiers used to describe vulnerabilities.

4.1   Testing Approaches

Test tools employ several different analysis techniques including correctness testing, analysis of source code or binary code, use of static or dynamic analysis, and manual or automatic app testing.

4.1.1   Correctness Testing

One approach for testing an app is *software correctness testing* [18]. Software correctness testing is the process of executing a program to detect errors. Although the objective of software correctness testing is improving quality assurance as well as verifying and validating described functionality or estimating reliability, it also can help reveal potential security vulnerabilities that often can have a negative effect on the quality, functionality and reliability of the software. For example, software that crashes or exhibits unexpected behavior is often indicative of a security flaw. A prime advantage of software correctness testing is that it is traditionally based on specifications of the software to be tested. These specifications can be transformed into requirements that specify how the software is expected to behave while undergoing testing. This is distinguished from security assessment approaches that often require the tester to derive requirements themselves; often such requirements are largely based on security requirements that are common across many different software artifacts and may not test for vulnerabilities that are unique to the software under test. Nonetheless, because of the tight coupling between security and quality, and functionality and reliability, it is recommended that software correctness testing be performed when possible.

4.1.2   Source and Binary Code Testing

A major factor in performing app testing is whether source code is available. Typically, apps downloaded from an app store do not come with access to source code. When source code is available, such as in the case of an open-source app, a variety of tools can be used to analyze it. The goals of a source code review are to find vulnerabilities in the source code and to verify the results of test tools. Even with automated aids, the analysis is labor-intensive. Benefits to using automated static analysis tools include introducing consistency between different reviews and making possible reviews of large codebases. Reviewers should generally use automated static analysis tools whether they are conducting an automated or a manual review and they should express their findings in terms of Common Weakness Enumeration (CWE) identifiers or some other widely accepted nomenclature. Performing a secure code review requires software development and domain-specific knowledge in the area of app security. Organizations should ensure the individuals performing source code reviews have the required skills and expertise.

Organizations that intend to develop apps in-house also should refer to guidance on secure programming techniques and software quality assurance processes to appropriately address the entire software development lifecycle [19] [20].

When an app's source code is not available, its binary code can be analyzed instead. In the context of apps, the term "binary code" can refer to either byte-code or machine code. For example, Android apps are compiled to byte code that is executed on a virtual machine, similar to the Java Virtual Machine (JVM), but they can also come with custom libraries that are provided in the form of machine code, i.e., code executed directly on a mobile device's CPU. Android binary apps include byte-code that can be analyzed without hardware support using emulated and virtual environments.

4.1.3　Static and Dynamic Testing

Analysis tools are often characterized as either static or dynamic.[11] Static analysis examines the app source code and binary code and attempts to reason all possible behaviors that might arise at runtime. It provides a level of assurance that analysis results accurately describe the program's behavior regardless of the input or execution environment. Dynamic analysis operates by executing a program using a set of input use-cases and analyzing the program's runtime behavior. In some cases, the enumeration of input test cases is large, resulting in lengthy processing times. However, methods such as combinatorial testing can reduce the number of dynamic input test case combinations, reducing the amount of time needed to derive analysis results [22]. However, dynamic analysis is unlikely to provide 100 percent code coverage [23]. Organizations should consider the technical tradeoff differences between what static and dynamic tools offer and balance their usage given the organization's software assurance goals.

Static analysis requires that binary code be reverse engineered when source code is not available, which is relatively easy for byte code[12] but can be difficult for machine code. Many commercial static analysis tools already support bytecode as do a number of open-source and academic tools.[13] For machine code, it is especially hard to track the flow of control across many functions and to track data flow through variables, since most variables are stored in anonymous memory locations that can be accessed in different ways. The most common way to reverse engineer machine code is to use a disassembler or a decompiler that attempts to recover the original source code. These techniques are especially useful if the purpose of reverse engineering is to allow humans to examine the code because the outputs are in a form that can be understood by humans with appropriate skills. However, even the best disassemblers make mistakes [25]. If the code is being reverse engineered for static analysis, it is preferable to disassemble the machine code directly to a form that the static analyzer understands rather than creating human-readable code as an intermediate byproduct. A static analysis tool aimed at machine code is likely to automate this process.

---

[11]　For mobile devices, there are analysis tools that label themselves as performing behavioral testing. Behavioral testing (also known as behavioral analysis) is a form of static and dynamic testing that attempts to detect malicious or risky behavior such as the oft-cited example of a flashlight app that accesses a contact list [21]. This publication assumes that any mention of static or dynamic testing also includes behavioral testing as a subset of its capabilities.

[12]　The ASM framework [24] is a commonly used framework for byte code analysis.

[13]　Such as [24–27].

In contrast to static analysis, the most important dynamic analysis requirement is to see the workings of the code as it is being executed. There are two primary ways to obtain this information. First, an executing app can be connected to a remote debugger. Second, the code can be run on an emulator that has built-in debugging capabilities. Running the code on the intended mobile device allows the test tool to select the exact characteristics of the device and can provide a more accurate view about how the app will be behave. On the other hand, an emulator provides more control, especially when the emulator is open-source and can be modified by the evaluator to capture whatever information is needed. Although emulators can simulate different devices, they do not simulate all of them and therefore the simulation may not be completely accurate. Note that malware increasingly detects the use of emulators as a testing platform and changes its behavior accordingly to avoid detection. Therefore, it is recommended that test tools use a combination of emulated and physical mobile devices to avoid false-negatives from malware that employs anti-detection techniques.

Useful information can be gleaned by observing an app's behavior even without knowing the purposes of individual functions. For example, a test tool can observe how the app interacts with its external resources, recording the services it requests from the operating system and the permissions it exercises. Although many of the device capabilities used by an app may be inferred by a test tool (e.g., access to a device's camera will be required of a camera app), an app may be permitted access to additional device capabilities that are beyond the scope of its described functionality (e.g., a camera app accessing the device's network). Moreover, if the behavior of the app is observed for specific inputs, the evaluator can ask whether the capabilities being exercised make sense in the context of those particular inputs. For example, a calendar app may legitimately have permission to send calendar data across the network to sync across multiple devices, but if the user merely has asked for a list of the day's appointments and the app sends data that is not part of the handshaking process needed to retrieve data, the test tool might investigate what data is being sent and for what purpose.

4.2 Vulnerability Classifiers and Quantifiers

It is advantageous to use a common language to describe vulnerabilities in mobile apps. The following sections describe some of the more commonly used classifiers and quantifiers used to identify, describe, and measure the severity of vulnerabilities.

4.2.1 Common Weakness Enumeration (CWE)

CWE is a software weakness classification system maintained by the MITRE Corporation [28]. CWE serves as a common language of sorts for software weakness categories. Different programming languages can create language-specific versions of the same software error. CWE ensures terminology exists to refer to the same error across disparate languages and offers mitigation strategies for each. The CWE is used worldwide in industry, government and academia.

4.2.2 Common Vulnerabilities and Exposures (CVE)

The CVE dictionary is a naming scheme for software vulnerabilities [12] that also is hosted by MITRE. When a vulnerability is identified, it can be reported to a CVE Numbering Authority, which provides a unique, industrywide identifier for the vulnerability. CVEs are reported to the

NVD for scoring and description. The NVD is the U.S. government repository of standards-based vulnerability management data and collects, analyzes and stores data describing specific computer system vulnerabilities. Additionally, the NVD hosts databases of security checklists, security-related software flaws, misconfigurations, product names, and impact metrics. NVD extensively uses the CWE as well as the CVE to accomplish its mission.

4.2.3   Common Vulnerability Scoring System (CVSS)

The Common Vulnerability Scoring System Version (CVSS) is a vulnerability scoring system owned and maintained by the Forum of Incident Response and Security Teams (FIRST) [29]. The CVSS model attempts to ensure repeatable and accurate measurement, while enabling users to view the underlying vulnerability characteristics used to generate numerical scores. This common measurement system can be used by industries, organizations and governments that require accurate and consistent vulnerability exploit and impact scores. The algorithm used to calculate vulnerability scores is open to all and is derived principally by human analyst-provided inputs for three metric categories: base, temporal and environmental. Common uses of CVSS are calculating the severity and prioritization of vulnerability remediation activities. The NVD provides vulnerability scores via the CVSS.

5   App Vetting Considerations

This section describes additional criteria that organizations should consider when establishing their app vetting processes.

5.1   Managed and Unmanaged Apps

Enterprise applications, or third-party applications deployed on enterprise devices (or personal devices used for enterprise tasks), may be managed throughout the deployment lifecycle, from initial deployment and configuration through removal of the app from a device. Administering such managed applications can be performed using enterprise Mobile Application Management (MAM) systems which are designed to enable enterprise control over mobile applications that access enterprise services and/or data. Unmanaged (personal use) applications are applications that are not administered by MAM (or similar) systems.

One benefit of managing only applications (as opposed to the entire device) is that MAM systems do not require the user/owner to enroll the entire device under enterprise management, nor must the owner accept installation of an enterprise profile on the device. MAM solutions can enable an enterprise to integrate an in-house enterprise applications catalog with a mobile device vendor's App Store (e.g., Apple's App Store, Google Play, or the Microsoft Store) to allow mobile users to easily install an enterprise app. Enterprise system administrators may be able to deploy apps or push out over-the-air app updates to mobile users; they may also be able to restrict app functionalities without affecting the entire device, which may be preferred by Bring Your Own Device (BYOD) users. Some Mobile Device Management (MDM) systems also include MAM functionality, enabling fine grained control over different applications on a single managed device. MDM and MAM features can be used to restrict flow of enterprise data between managed and unmanaged applications.

An enterprise should consider the tradeoffs between managed and unmanaged apps when designing its mobility solutions, requirements, and policies for managing mobile applications (examples of such security requirements can be found in the DoD Chief Information Officer memo on "Mobile Application Security Requirements" [30]). Tradeoffs may include the administrative overhead and extra cost versus the security guarantees obtained by allowing only managed apps on mobile devices that access enterprise networks and services.

5.2   App Whitelisting and App Blacklisting

Application whitelisting and blacklisting refers to allowing or disallowing the use of applications based on a pre-specified list to protect against installation of malicious, vulnerable, or flawed applications. NIST SP 800-53 Rev. 4 [31] defines these control enhancements under configuration management (CM) control number CM-7, least functionality, as follows:

- Enhancement CM-7 (4) Least Functionality, Unauthorized Software–Blacklisting is an allow-all, deny-by-exception policy that prohibits the execution of unauthorized software programs on a system. Blacklisting requires the organization to develop and maintain a list of unauthorized software (apps)

- Enhancement CM-7 (5) Least Functionality, Unauthorized Software–Whitelisting is a deny-all, permit-by-exception policy to allow the execution of only authorized software programs on the system. This requires the organization to develop and maintain a list of authorized software (apps)

Both whitelisting and blacklisting can be augmented and facilitated via MAM/MDM software. For federal organizations it is important to note at the time of this document's publication, 800-53 Rev. 4 recommends blacklisting for systems in the moderate baseline allocation and whitelisting for systems with high baseline allocation. Future revisions of 800-53[14] may also recommend blacklisting and whitelisting in both the moderate and high baseline allocations.

5.3 App Vetting Limitations

As with any software assurance process, there is no guarantee that even the most thorough vetting process will uncover all potential vulnerabilities or malicious behavior. Organizations should be made aware that although app security assessments generally improve the security posture of the organization, the degree to which they do so may not be easily or immediately ascertained. Organizations should also be made aware of what the vetting process does and does not provide in terms of security.

Organizations should also be educated on the value of humans in security assessment processes and ensure that their app vetting does not rely solely on automated tests. Security analysis is primarily a human-driven process [19] [32]; automated tools by themselves cannot address many of the contextual and nuanced interdependencies that underlie software security. The most obvious reason for this is that fully understanding software behavior is one of the classic impossible problems of computer science [33], and in fact current technology has not even reached the limits of what is theoretically possible. Complex, multifaceted software architectures cannot be fully analyzed by automated means.

Additionally, current software analysis tools do not inherently understand what software has to do to behave in a secure manner in a particular context. For example, failure to encrypt data transmitted to the cloud may not be a security issue if the transmission is tunneled through a virtual private network (VPN). Even if the security requirements for an app have been correctly predicted and are completely understood, there is no current technology for unambiguously translating human-readable requirements into a form that can be understood by machines.

For these reasons, security analysis requires human analysts be in the loop, and by extension the quality of the outcome depends, among other things, on the level of human effort and expertise available for an evaluation. Analysts should be familiar with standard processes and best practices for software security assessment [19] [34–36]. In order to be successful, a robust app vetting process should use a toolbox approach where multiple assessment tools and processes, as well as human interaction work together. Reliance on only a single tool, even with human interaction, is a significant risk because of the inherent limitations of each tool.

---

[14] https://csrc.nist.gov/publications/detail/sp/800-53/rev-5/draft

5.4 Local and Remote Tools and Services

There are many tools and services dedicated to analyzing mobile apps [37] [38]. Depending on the model employed by the tool/service provider, app analysis may occur in different physical locations. For example, an analysis tool may be installed and run within the network of the organization for whom the app is intended. Other vendors may host their test services offsite. Offsite tools may reside on premise of the tool/service provider or may reside in a cloud infrastructure. Each of these scenarios should be understood by an organization prior to employing a vetting tool/service, especially in those cases where the app's code base may contain sensitive or classified information.

5.5 Automated Approval/Rejection

In some cases, the activities conducted by analysts to derive recommendations for approving or rejecting an app can be automated, particularly if no organization-specific policies, regulation, etc. are required. Here, an app vetting system used to support the specification of rules can be configured to automatically approve or reject an app based on risk assessments from multiple tools. For example, an app vetting system could be configured to automatically recommend an app if all test tools deem the app as having "LOW" risk. Similarly, an app vetting system could be configured to automatically enforce organization-specific requirements. For example, using metadata extracted during the preprocessing of an app, an app vetting system could automatically reject an app from a specific vendor.

5.6 Reciprocity

Reciprocity involves sharing results across app vetting teams to reduce re-work; it occurs when a federal agency's app vetting process leverages results from another agency that has previously performed app vetting on the same app [39]. It enables the receiving agency to reuse the app testing results when making their own risk determination on deployment of the app. To share the security vetting results, the testing agency captures the results of app security testing against a common set of security requirements (e.g., NIAP) in a standardized reciprocity report format, with the intention to make the information available for use by other agencies.

Given the different potential uses any individual app may have and different mobile architectures between different agencies, sharing risk decisions (approval/rejection) is not recommended. The alternative is to make findings from tests conducted by one federal agency available to other federal agencies, allowing agencies to make their own risk-based determinations without having to repeat tests already conducted by other agencies. This sharing of an organization's findings for an app can greatly reduce the duplication and cost of app vetting efforts for other organizations. Information sharing within the software assurance community is vital and can help test tools benefit from the collective efforts of security professionals around the world. The National Vulnerability Database (NVD) [40] is the U.S. government repository of standards-based vulnerability management data represented using the Security Content Automation Protocol (SCAP) [41]. This data enables automation of vulnerability management, security measurement, and compliance. The NVD includes databases of security checklists, security-related software flaws, misconfigurations, product names, and impact metrics. SCAP is a suite of specifications that standardize the format and nomenclature by which security software products communicate software flaw and security configuration information. SCAP is a multipurpose protocol that supports automated vulnerability checking, technical control compliance activities, and security measurements. Goals for the development of SCAP include standardizing system security management, promoting interoperability of security products, and fostering the use of standard expressions of security content. The CWE [28] and Common Attack Pattern Enumeration and Classification (CAPEC) [42] collections can provide a useful list of weaknesses and attack approaches to drive a binary or live system penetration test. Classifying and expressing software vulnerabilities is an ongoing and developing effort in the software assurance community, as is how to prioritize among the various weaknesses that can be in an app so that an organization can know that those that pose the most danger to the app, given its intended use/mission, are addressed by the vetting activity given the difference in the effectiveness and coverage of the various available tools and techniques.

5.7   Tool Report Analysis

One issue related to report and risk analysis stems from the difficulty in collating, normalizing and interpreting different reports and risk assessments due to the wide variety of security-related definitions, semantics, nomenclature and metrics used by different test tools. For example, one test tool may classify the estimated risk for using an app as low, moderate, high or severe risk, while another may classify the estimated risk as pass, warning or fail. While some standards exist for expressing risk assessment[15] and vulnerability reporting[16] the current adoption of these standards by test tools is low. To the extent possible, it is recommended that an organization use test tools that leverage vulnerability reporting and risk assessment standards. If this approach is not possible, it is recommended that the organization provide sufficient training to analysts on the interpretation of reports and risk assessments generated by test tools.

5.8   Compliance versus Certification

For mobile application vetting, two terms are frequently used to demonstrate proof of successful implementation of mobile app security requirements. For a mobile application that has been developed to include security aimed at a particular requirement (e.g. National Information Assurance Partnership – Requirements for Vetting Mobile Apps from the Protection Profile for Application Software [7]) developers may choose to note that they are compliant or certified. The difference depends on the organization's need for compliance or certification.

Compliance for mobile application security means either self-attestation or attestation from an unofficial third party that has validated the mobile app meets such security requirements. For example an enterprise may choose to use their own internally developed mobile application vetting process to validate the security and privacy of a mobile application. By going through their own internal process they approve the mobile application for use in their organization or on

---

[15] An example standard, the Common Vulnerability Scoring System CVSS, is discussed in Section4.2.3.

[16] Examples are described in Section 2.1.

their organization's mobile assets.

On the other hand, certification means successful validation from the authorized validator. For example, for NIAP certification, a formal NIAP validation process must be followed.[17] In this case, vendors may choose an approved Common Criterial Testing Lab to conduct the product evaluation against an applicable NIAP-approved Protection Profile. Following successful completion of the validation process, a formal certification would be granted and listed on an approved product list.

NIAP lists products on a product-compliant list [43] when a certification has been successfully granted. This is an official list and requires NIAP's official certification for use in federal information systems. It should be noted that the certification requirements evaluated by NIAP certification may not map directly into non-federal requirements. In the case of regulated industries, such as the financial and health industries, it is important that organizations should follow their respective compliance requirements as appropriate. This distinction may also extend to state and local organizations as well.

5.9   Budget and Staffing

App software assurance activity costs should be included in project budgets and should not be an afterthought. Such costs may be significant and can include licensing costs for test tools and salaries for analysts, approvers, and administrators. Organizations that hire contractors to develop apps should specify that app assessment costs be included as part of the app development process. Note, however, that for apps developed in-house, attempting to implement app vetting solely at the end of the development effort will lead to increased costs and lengthened project timelines. It is strongly recommended to identify potential vulnerabilities or weaknesses during the development process when they can still be addressed by the original developers. Identifying and fixing errors during the development process is also significantly cheaper than fixing errors once a product is released [44].

To provide an optimal app vetting process implementation, it is critical for the organization to hire personnel with appropriate expertise. For example, organizations should hire analysts experienced in software security and information assurance as well as administrators experienced in mobile security.

---

[17] https://www.niap-ccevs.org/Ref/Evals.cfm

6   App Vetting Systems

While an app vetting process may be performed manually, it is typically advantageous to perform an app vetting process in a semi-or full-automated fashion using an app vetting system (e.g., the DHS AppVet system [16]). An app vetting system is a system that manages and automates an app vetting process and may be implemented as a web-based service and is typically part of a larger app vetting ecosystem that comprises test tools/services, app stores, EMMs, and users.

An app vetting system is used by a security analyst (often an enterprise system administrator) to identify app security issues before an app is deployed to a user's mobile device. After the system analyzes the app, the security analyst considers the vetting results within the context of the security posture of the larger enterprise environment and makes a security recommendation. An authorizing official then decides whether to approve the use of the app, given the user's role, the mission need addressed by the app, and the security recommendation of the security analyst. Figure 7 depicts a reference architecture for an app vetting system.

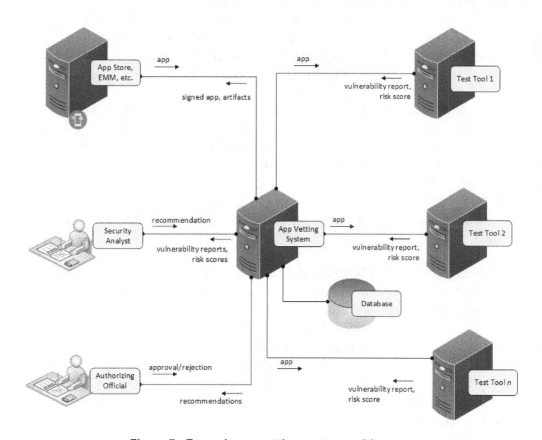

Figure 7 - Example app vetting system architecture.

At the center of the diagram is the app vetting system. This system is the central hub to the larger app vetting ecosystem. The app vetting system coordinates requests and responses among all the other system components, the security analyst and the authorizing official. A crucial component and function of the vetting system is that it serves as the long-term memory and decision repository for the app vetting process. In the diagram, this is represented by the database symbol connected to the app vetting system. This database should store testing reports as well as the inputs of the security analyst and authorizing official for posterity.

An enterprise mobile device seeking to use an app may do so in several ways. The enterprise may host a specific app store that only contains vetted applications. Alternately, the device may have policy rules enforced by an enterprise mobility management (EMM) system that regulates what apps may be installed from any source. These systems are represented by the box in the upper left corner of the diagram. Information about the requested app (usually app binary code, but sometimes app source code for apps developed "in house") is sent from this system to the app vetting coordination hub to begin the app vetting process

There are many different strategies for examining an app and evaluating its security characteristics. No single algorithm, tool or product offers a complete picture of an app's security characteristics. The reference architecture shows how an organization might take input from multiple (three are shown at right in the figure) test tools to better inform the security analyst. After the request for app vetting is sent from the App Store or EMM system to the vetting hub, the hub contacts each of the three test tools in the diagram. Each tool receives a copy of the information provided about the app (e.g., binary or source code), performs its independent assessment and returns a vulnerability report and some form of risk score.

The vetting hub then gathers the results reported by the various test tools, potentially summarizing those results and offering them to the security analyst in a dashboard view. After reviewing the results of the various tests, the security analyst submits a recommendation, which is recorded by the vetting hub. The authorizing official can then consider the security analyst's recommendation together with mission needs to approve or reject the use of the app by the mobile user. If the app is approved for installation, the vetting hub can provide digitally-signed artifacts, including digitally-signed apps, back to the App Store or EMM system to enable the app deployment.

While the figure depicts a locally hosted app vetting system (i.e., the app vetting hub, test tools, database and App Store are shown as residing on hosts), many app vetting systems may be hosted in a cloud environment. In a cloud-hosted scenario, the boxes shown in the diagram would be hosted by a private or public cloud service provider and much of the functionality would be virtualized. The security analyst and authorizing official need not know how the vetting system is implemented. In either type of deployment, users in these roles would interact with the system through a dashboard providing the appropriate services and views. Both types of deployment enable modular extension of the app vetting system to accommodate new vetting test tools as these become available.

An app vetting system uses application programming interfaces (APIs), network protocols and schemas to integrate with distributed third-party test tools as well as clients including app stores. An app vetting system may also include a user interface (UI) dashboard that allows users such as administrators, analysts and authorizing officials to view reports and risk assessments, provide recommendations and approve or reject apps. Figure 7 shows an example of how an app vetting system utilizing APIs and a UI can be used to support integration with all components and users in an app vetting ecosystem.

Appendix A—Threats to Mobile Applications

Like all software, mobile apps often contain vulnerabilities (introduced by errors in design or implementation or by malicious intent) that can expose a user, a mobile device and its data or enterprise services or its data to attacks. There are a number of common classes of mobile software errors that can create such vulnerabilities, including errors in the use or implementation of cryptographic primitives and other security services, risky interactions among software components on a mobile device, and risky interactions between the mobile device and systems within its environment. Common errors in using security services or cryptography include weak authentication of users or systems, incorrect implementation of cryptographic primitives, choosing outdated or broken cryptographic algorithms or parameters, or failure to encrypt app traffic between a mobile device and web- or enterprise-hosted services. Risky interactions among software components on a mobile device include the use of data from untrustworthy sources as input to security-sensitive operations, use of vulnerable third-party-provided software libraries, and app code that leaks sensitive data outside of the app (e.g., through logs of app activity). Also, mobile systems may be exposed to malicious code or injections of data through communication with a compromised web or enterprise service.

Vetting mobile apps before deploying them onto a user's mobile device can enable an enterprise system administrator to detect software or configuration flaws that may create vulnerabilities or violate enterprise security or privacy policies. Mobile app vetting systems typically include automated testing and analysis tools and may interact with externally hosted vetting services. This section will discuss different classes of malware that affect mobile devices. Mobile app vetting systems are designed to look for evidence of such malware.

It is important to recognize the constantly shifting attack landscape while considering the following classes of mobile application threats. This list is not intended to be exhaustive, nor should it be taken a conclusive and/or prescriptive rubric to evaluate the strength of a vetting solution, legislation, or security posture. Rather, it is intended to be an illustrative list of currently *observed* threats.

A.1   Ransomware

Ransomware is malware that encrypts data and holds the decryption key hostage for payment [45]. In the mobile environment, new ransomware [46] has been observed that not only encrypts the data of users, but also locks them out of their devices by changing the lock screen PIN. Such ransomware has been spreading as a fake software updates via compromised websites.

A.2   Spyware

Spyware [47] is malware designed to gather information about an individual or organization without their knowledge and send that information to the attacker's systems. While spyware often has been used to track internet user's movements on the Web, it may also be used to capture short messing service (SMS) messages, photos, phone call logs or sensitive data such as user logins or banking information. Most spyware is installed without a device user's (or the organization's) knowledge, often using deceptive tactics that trick the user into installation. Nation-state actors also have used spyware to gather information from mobile users [48].

A.3   Adware

Adware is malware that is embedded within or loaded as part of advertisements and is one of the most common threats to mobile devices worldwide. Mobile ads are instrumental to the current mobile ecosystem because they provide a source of funding for software developers that offer free mobile apps. Ads may be served from third-party websites and may contain that often is used to capture personal information without a user's permission or knowledge. Recent reports [49] have shown some low-end mobile devices were shipped from the manufacturer with adware pre-installed. Users with affected phones experience popup ads and other annoying problems and because the adware is installed at the firmware level it is incredibly difficult to remove.

A.4   Rooting

"Rooting" is the process of enabling users to gain privileged (root) access on the device's operating system (OS)[18]. Rooting is often performed to overcome restrictions that carriers and device manufacturers enforce on some mobile devices. Rooting enables alteration or replacement of a system's applications and settings, execution of specialized apps requiring administrative privileges, or performance of carrier-prohibited operations. There are two types of rooting [50]

- "Soft rooting" typically is performed via a third-party application that uses a security vulnerability called a "root exploit".
- "Hard rooting" requires flashing binary executables and provides super-user privileges.

On some mobile platforms (e.g., Android), techniques beyond rooting exist which unlock the device bootloader to facilitate the complete removal and replacement of the device's OS, e.g., to install a newer or modified version of it.

A.5   Trojan Horse

A Trojan horse (or a Trojan) is malware that poses as legitimate and often familiar software, thereby tricking a user into running it. For traditional computing platforms, attackers typically hide malware using file names with well-known extensions, such as .doc or .jpg. Users open the Trojan file and the malware begins to execute. In the mobile environment, mobile banking Trojans are a worrisome new trend [51] that describes malware installed after victims respond to a phishing message that appears to be from their bank. The malware gathers financial information, login credentials and sometimes credit card information.

A.6   Infostealer

An infostealer is a Trojan horse that gathers information, including confidential data, from an infected system and sends it to an attacker's system. The most common types of information stolen include user credentials (e.g., login user name and password) or financial data. Infostealers commonly have affected traditional computing platforms but have more recently begun impacting

---

[18] Note, the term *jailbreaking* is commonly used in industry to describe rooting an iOS device.

mobile platforms. Recent reports [52] describe malware that poses as a Google Chrome update for Android devices and disables antivirus applications. The malware can harvest user banking information, call logs, SMS data and browser history, which are sent to remote servers.

A.7   Hostile Downloader

A Hostile Downloader is malware whose primary purpose is to download content, usually from the Internet. Downloaded content may often include other malicious apps (which often are launched by the downloader), configurations or commands for the downloader or for other software installed on the system, and additional software components to facilitate an attack. For example, in 2017, attackers used a malicious PowerPoint presentation embedded in a spam email to launch a banking Trojan [53]. Opening the PowerPoint file and just hovering the mouse pointer over a displayed hyperlink—no clicking required–caused PowerPoint to execute a malicious script that downloaded a Trojan horse.

A.8   SMS Fraud

Scams once perpetrated via email now are perpetrated via SMS messaging. Fraudulent business transactions, phishing (called "smishing" when delivered via SMS messages), phony requests for donations, fees to claim lottery prizes and cons originating from dating sites are all SMS scams [54]. Users must be wary of unsolicited texts from strangers or unknown numbers, especially requests for money or personal/sensitive information.

A.9   Call Fraud

Call fraud refers to several malicious and illegal activities. For example, some users of cellular services may receive calls that appear to originate from domestic area codes but are actually associated with international pay-per-call services. These calls often disconnect after one ring. When the target returns the call he or she is connected to an international line that charges a fee for connecting in addition to significant per-minute fees if the victim stays on the line. These charges usually show up on the victim's cellular bill as premium services.

A.10 Man in the Middle Attack (MITM)

A Man in the Middle attack (MiTM) is defined simply as any method of intercepting communication between two systems [55]. Mobile applications are specifically vulnerable to these types of attacks because the misuse/misconfiguration of the primary defense against it: Transport Layer Security (TLS). The acceptance of untrusted SSL certificates, permitting the use of weaker TLS modes, and vulnerabilities in the trust model itself can leave a mobile application vulnerable to MiTM attacks leading to potential information leaks and privacy violations.

A.11   Toll Fraud

Toll fraud occurs when a mobile device user makes a call—often using premium services—that is charged to a third-party that did not authorize the call. A common attack involves a hacker leasing phone numbers from a web-based service that charges callers for each call and provides a percentage of the profit to the hacker. To make a lucrative fraud-based business, the hacker breaches an independent business's Voice Over IP (VoIP) network to forward calls to the hacker's premium service numbers. The independent company is billed for the calls by the web-based service and the hacker gets a percentage of the profits. To resist these type of attacks, organizations must implement strong network security protections.

Appendix B—Android App Vulnerability Types

This appendix identifies vulnerabilities specific to apps running on Android mobile devices. The scope of this appendix includes app vulnerabilities for Android-based mobile devices running apps written in Java. The scope does not include vulnerabilities in the mobile platform hardware and communications networks. Although some of the vulnerabilities described below are common across mobile device environments, this appendix focuses only on Android-specific vulnerabilities.

The vulnerabilities in this appendix are broken into three hierarchical levels, A, B, and C. The A level is referred to as the vulnerability class and is the broadest description for the vulnerabilities specified under that level. The B level is referred to as the sub-class and attempts to narrow down the scope of the vulnerability class into a smaller, common group of vulnerabilities. The C level specifies the individual vulnerabilities that have been identified. The purpose of this hierarchy is to guide the reader to finding the type of vulnerability they are looking for as quickly as possible.

Table 3 shows the A level general categories of Android app vulnerabilities.

Table 3 - Android Vulnerabilities, A Level.

Type	Description	Negative Consequence
Incorrect Permissions	Permissions allow accessing controlled functionality such as the camera or Global Positioning System (GPS) and are requested in the program. Permissions can be implicitly granted to an app without the user's consent.	An app with too many permissions may perform unintended functions outside the scope of the app's intended functionality. Additionally, the permissions are vulnerable to hijacking by another app. If too few permissions are granted, the app will not be able to perform the functions required.
Exposed Communications	Internal communications protocols are the means by which an app passes messages internally within the device, either to itself or to other apps. External communications allow information to leave the device.	Exposed internal communications allow apps to gather unintended information and inject new information. Exposed external communication (data network, Wi-Fi, Bluetooth, Near-Field Communication (NFC), *etc.*) leave information open to disclosure or man-in-the-middle attacks.
Exposed Data Storage	Files created by apps on Android can be stored in Internal Storage, External Storage, or the Keystore. Files stored in External Storage may be read and modified by all other apps with the External Storage permission.	Sensitive data can be exfiltrated or tampered by other apps, or unintentionally transferred to another system in a backup. It should be noted, there are cases when apps require this behavior to function as intended.
Potentially Dangerous Functionality	Controlled functionality that accesses system-critical resources or the user's personal information. This functionality can be invoked through API calls or hard coded into an app.	Unintended functions could be performed outside the scope of the app's functionality.
App Collusion	Two or more apps passing information to each other in order to increase the capabilities of one or both apps beyond their declared scope.	Collusion can allow apps to obtain data that was unintended such as a gaming app obtaining access to the user's contact list.

Type	Description	Negative Consequence
Obfuscation	Functionality or control flows that are hidden or obscured from the user. For the purposes of this appendix, obfuscation was defined as three criteria: external library calls, reflection, and native code usage.	1. External libraries can contain unexpected and/or malicious functionality. 2. Reflective calls can obscure the control flow of an app and/or subvert permissions within an app. 3. Native code (code written in languages other than Java in Android) can perform unexpected and/or malicious functionality.
Excessive Power Consumption	Excessive functions or unintended apps running on a device which intentionally or unintentionally drain the battery.	Shortened battery life could affect the ability to perform mission-critical functions.
Traditional Software Vulnerabilities	All vulnerabilities associated with traditional Java code including: Authentication and Access Control, Buffer Handling, Control Flow Management, Encryption and Randomness, Error Handling, File Handling, Information Leaks, Initialization and Shutdown, Injection, Malicious Logic, Number Handling, and Pointer and Reference Handling.	Common consequences include unexpected outputs, resource exhaustion, denial of service, *etc.*

Table 4 shows the hierarchy of Android app vulnerabilities from A level to C level.

Table 4 - Android Vulnerabilities by level.

Level A	Level B	Level C
Incorrect Permissions	Over Granting	Over Granting in Code
		Over Granting in API
	Under Granting	Under Granting in Code
		Under Granting in API
	Developer Created Permissions	Developer Created in Code
		Developer Created in API
	Implicit Permission	Granted through API
		Granted through Other Permissions
		Granted through Grandfathering
Exposed Communications	External Communications	Bluetooth
		GPS
		Network/Data Communications
		NFC Access
	Internal Communications	Unprotected Intents
		Unprotected Activities
		Unprotected Services
		Unprotected Content Providers
		Unprotected Broadcast Receivers
		Debug Flag
Exposed Data Storage	Over Exposing Data	
		Over exposing data as world readable in

Level A	Level B	Level C
		internal storage
Potentially Dangerous Functionality	Direct Addressing	Memory Access
		Internet Access
	Potentially Dangerous API	Cost Sensitive APIs
		Personal Information APIs
		Device Management APIs
	Privilege Escalation	Altering File Privileges
		Accessing Super User/Root
App Collusion	Content Provider/Intents	Unprotected Content Providers
		Permission Protected Content Providers
		Pending Intents
	Broadcast Receiver	Broadcast Receiver for Critical Messages
	Data Creation/Changes/Deletion	Creation/Changes/Deletion to File Resources
		Creation/Changes/Deletion to Database Resources
	Number of Services	Excessive Checks for Service State
Obfuscation	Library Calls	Use of Potentially Dangerous Libraries
		Potentially Malicious Libraries Packaged but Not Used
	Native Code Detection	
	Reflection	
	Packed Code	
Excessive Power Consumption	CPU Usage	
	I/O	

Appendix C—iOS App Vulnerability Types

This appendix identifies and defines the various types of vulnerabilities that are specific to apps running on mobile devices utilizing the Apple iOS operating system. The scope does not include vulnerabilities in the mobile platform hardware and communications networks. Although some of the vulnerabilities described below are common across mobile device environments, this appendix focuses on iOS-specific vulnerabilities.

The vulnerabilities in this appendix are broken into three hierarchical levels, A, B, and C. The A level is referred to as the vulnerability class and is the broadest description for the vulnerabilities specified under that level. The B level is referred to as the sub-class and attempts to narrow down the scope of the vulnerability class into a smaller, common group of vulnerabilities. The C level specifies the individual vulnerabilities that have been identified. The purpose of this hierarchy is to guide the reader to finding the type of vulnerability they are looking for as quickly as possible.

Table 5 shows the A level general categories of iOS app vulnerabilities.

Table 5 - iOS Vulnerability Descriptions, A Level.

Type	Description	Negative Consequence
Incorrect Permissions	Permissions allow accessing controlled functionality such as the camera or GPS and are requested in the program. Permissions can be implicitly granted to an app without the user's consent.	An app with too many permissions may perform unintended functions outside the scope of the app's intended functionality. Additionally, the permissions are vulnerable to hijacking by another app. If too few permissions are granted, the app will not be able to perform the functions required.
Exposed Communication- Internal and External	Internal communications protocols allow apps to process information and communicate with other apps. External communications allow information to leave the device.	Exposed internal communications allow apps to gather unintended information and inject new information. Exposed external communication (data network, Wi-Fi, Bluetooth, *etc.*) leave information open to disclosure or man-in-the-middle attacks.
Potentially Dangerous Functionality	Controlled functionality that accesses system-critical resources or the user's personal information. This functionality can be invoked through API calls or hard coded into an app.	Unintended functions could be performed outside the scope of the app's functionality.
App Collusion	Two or more apps passing information to each other in order to increase the capabilities of one or both apps beyond their declared scope.	Collusion can allow apps to obtain data that was unintended such as a gaming app obtaining access to the user's contact list.
Obfuscation	Functionality or control flow that is hidden or obscured from the user. For the purposes of this appendix, obfuscation was defined as three criteria: external library calls, reflection, and packed code.	1. External libraries can contain unexpected and/or malicious functionality. 2. Reflective calls can obscure the control flow of an app and/or subvert permissions within an app. 3. Packed code prevents code reverse engineering and can be used to hide malware.

Type	Description	Negative Consequence
Excessive Power Consumption	Excessive functions or unintended apps running on a device which intentionally or unintentionally drain the battery.	Shortened battery life could affect the ability to perform mission-critical functions.
Traditional Software Vulnerabilities	All vulnerabilities associated with Objective C and others. This includes: Authentication and Access Control, Buffer Handling, Control Flow Management, Encryption and Randomness, Error Handling, File Handling, Information Leaks, Initialization and Shutdown, Injection, Malicious Logic, Number Handling and Pointer and Reference Handling.	Common consequences include unexpected outputs, resource exhaustion, denial of service, *etc.*
Exposed Data Storage	All files and keychain items on iOS are assigned Data Protection classes. These dictate whether the item is 1) accessible while the device is locked, 2) accessible when the associated app is closed, and 3) if the item can be transferred to another device.	Sensitive data can be less protected on the file system while not being used, or unintentionally transferred to another system in a backup. However, restricting the use of this mechanism may impair an app's ability to perform desired functionality

Table 6 shows the hierarchy of iOS app vulnerabilities from A level to C level.

Table 6 - iOS Vulnerabilities by level.

Level A	Level B	Level C
Incorrect Permissions	Sensitive Information	Contacts
		Calendar Information
		Tasks
		Reminders
		Photos
		Bluetooth Access
Exposed Communications	External Communications	Telephony
		Bluetooth
		GPS
		SMS/MMS
		Network/Data Communications
	Internal Communications	Abusing Protocol Handlers
Potentially Dangerous Functionality	Direct Memory Mapping	Memory Access
		File System Access
	Potentially Dangerous API	Cost Sensitive APIs
		Device Management APIs
		Personal Information APIs
App Collusion	Data Change	Changes to Shared File Resources
		Changes to Shared Database Resources
		Changes to Shared Content Providers
	Data Creation/Deletion	Creation/Deletion to Shared File Resources

Level A	Level B	Level C
Obfuscation	Number of Services	Excessive Checks for Service State
	Native Code	Potentially Malicious Libraries Packaged but not Used
		Use of Potentially Dangerous Libraries
		Reflection Identification
		Class Introspection
	Library Calls	Constructor Introspection
		Field Introspection
		Method Introspection
	Packed Code	
Excessive Power Consumption	CPU Usage	
	I/O	
Exposed Data Storage	Over Exposing Data	Over Granting File Data Protection Class
		Over Granting Keychain Data Protection Class

Appendix D—Acronyms

Selected acronyms and abbreviations used in this paper are defined below

API	Application Programming Interface
BYOD	Bring Your Own Device
CAPEC	Common Attack Pattern Enumeration and Classification
CERT	Computer Emergency Response Team
CPU	Central Processing Unit
CVE	Common Vulnerabilities and Exposures
CWE	Common Weakness Enumeration
DHS	Department of Homeland Security
DoD	Department of Defense
EMM	Enterprise Mobility Management
GPS	Global Positioning System
IEEE	Institute of Electrical and Electronics Engineers
I/O	Input/Output
IoT	Internet of Things
ISO	International Organization for Standardization
ITL	Information Technology Laboratory
JVM	Java Virtual Machine
NFC	Near Field Communication
NIST	National Institute of Standards and Technology
NVD	National Vulnerability Database
OMB	Office of Management and Budget
PII	Personally Identifiable Information
PIN	Personal Identification Number

PIV	Personal Identity Verification
SAMATE	Software Assurance Metrics and Tool Evaluation
SCAP	Security Content Automation Protocol
SLA	Service Level Agreement
SP	Special Publication
UI	User Interface
VPN	Virtual Private Network
Wi-Fi	Wireless Fidelity.

Appendix E—Glossary

The definition of selected terms used in this publication are below

Analyst	A member of an organization who inspects reports and risk assessments from one or more test tools as well as organization-specific criteria to verify an app meets the organization's security requirements.
App Vetting Process	A sequence of activities performed by an organization to determine if a mobile app conforms to the organization's security requirements.
App Vetting System	A system for managing and automating an app vetting process.
Authorizing Official	An organization member who decides whether an app is approved or denied for use by the organization.
Dynamic Analysis	Detecting software vulnerabilities by executing an app using a set of input use-cases and analyzing the app's runtime behavior.
Enterprise Mobility Manager	A set of people, processes and technology focused on managing mobile devices, wireless networks and other mobile computing services in a business environment.
Functionality Testing	Verifying an app's user interface content and features perform and display as designed.
General App Security Requirements	The software and behavioral characteristics of an app that should or should not be present in order to ensure the security of the app.
Malware	Software or firmware intended to perform an unauthorized process that will have adverse impact on the confidentiality, integrity, or availability of an information system. A virus, worm, Trojan horse, or other code-based entity that infects a host. Spyware and some forms of adware are also examples of malicious code [31].
Mobile Device Management	The administration of mobile devices such as smartphones, tablet computers, laptops and desktop computers. MDM usually is implemented through a third-party product that has management features for particular vendors of mobile devices.

National Security System	Any information system, including any telecommunications system, used or operated by an agency or by a contractor of an agency or other organization on behalf of an agency:
	The function, operation or use of which--
	involves intelligence activities;
	involves cryptologic activities related to national security;
	involves command and control of military forces;
	involves equipment that is an integral part of a weapon or weapons system; or
	subject to subparagraph (B) is critical to the direct fulfillment of military or intelligence missions; or
	Is protected at all times by procedures established for information that have been specifically authorized under criteria established by an Executive Order or an Act of Congress to be kept classified in the interest of national defense or foreign policy [56].
Organization-Specific Security Requirements	Policies, regulations, and guidance that an organization must follow to ensure the security posture of an organization
Personally Identifiable Information	Information about an individual that can be used by a malicious actor to distinguish or trace the individual's identity and any other information that is linked or linkable to the individual [45].
Risk Assessment	A value that states a test tool's estimated level of security risk when an app is used. Risk assessments typically are based on the likelihood that a detected vulnerability will be exploited and the impact the detected vulnerability may have on the app or its related device or network. Risk assessments typically are represented as categories (e.g., low-, moderate- and high-risk).
Static Analysis	Detecting software vulnerabilities by examining an app's source code and binary and attempting to determine all possible behaviors that might arise at runtime.
Software Assurance	The level of confidence that software is free from vulnerabilities—either intentionally designed into the software or accidentally inserted during its lifecycle—and functions in the intended manner.

Software Correctness Testing	The process of executing a program to finding errors. The purpose of this testing is to improve quality assurance, verify and validate described functionality, or estimate reliability.
Software Vulnerability	A security flaw, glitch or weakness found in software that can be exploited by an attacker.
Test Tool	A tool or service that tests an app to determine if specific software vulnerabilities are present.

Appendix F—References

[1]   P. E. Black, L. Badger, B. Guttman, and E. Fong, *Dramatically Reducing Software Vulnerabilities: Report to the White House Office of Science and Technology Policy*, NIST IR 8151, National Institute of Standards and Technology, Gaithersburg, Maryland, November 2016. https://doi.org/10.6028/NIST.IR.8151

         National Institute of Standards and Technology, *Software Assurance*, Computer Security Resource Center: Glossary [Web site]. Available at https://csrc.nist.gov/glossary/term/software-assurance

[3]   M. Souppaya and K. Scarfone, *Guidelines for Managing the Security of Mobile Devices in the Enterprise*, NIST Special Publication (SP) 800-124 Revision 1, National Institute of Standards and Technology, Gaithersburg, Maryland, June 2013. https://doi.org/10.6028/NIST.SP.800-124r1

         Joint Task Force Transformation Initiative, *Security and Privacy Controls for Federal Information Systems and Organizations*, NIST Special Publication (SP) 800-53 Revision 4, National Institute of Standards and Technology, Gaithersburg, Maryland, April 2013 (including updates as of 01-15-2014), https://doi.org/10.6028/NIST.SP.800-53r4.

         International Organization for Standardization/International Electrotechnical Commission, *Information technology – Security techniques – Evaluation criteria for IT security – Part 1: Introduction and general model*, ISO/IEC 15408-1:2009, December 2009 (Corrected January 2014). Available at https://www.iso.org/standard/50341.html

         National Information Assurance Partnership, *Requirements for Vetting Mobile Apps from the Protection Profile for Application Software*, Version 1.2, April 22, 2016. Available at https://www.niap-ccevs.org/MMO/PP/394.R/pp_app_v1.2_table-reqs.htm

[8]   OWASP Foundation, *Mobile AppSec Verification*, Version 1.1.3, January 2019. Available at https://github.com/OWASP/owasp-masvs/releases/download/1.1.3/OWASP_Mobile_AppSec_Verification_Standard_1.1.3_Document.pdf

         OWASP Foundation, *Mobile Security Testing Guide (MSTG)*, 1.1.0 Release, November 30, 2018. Available at https://www.owasp.org/index.php/OWASP_Mobile_Security_Testing_Guide

[10]   M. Peck and C. Northern, *Analyzing the Effectiveness of App Vetting Tools in the Enterprise*, The MITRE Corporation, August 22, 2016. Available at https://www.mitre.org/sites/default/files/publications/pr-16-4772-analyzing-effectiveness-mobile-app-vetting-tools-report.pdf

Department of Homeland Security, *Build Security In*, US-CERT [Web site]. Available at https://www.us-cert.gov/bsi#ques

Joint Task Force Transformation Initiative, *Guide for Conducting Risk Assessments*, NIST Special Publication (SP) 800-30 Revision 1, National Institute of Standards and Technology, Gaithersburg, Maryland, September 2012. https://doi.org/10.6028/NIST.SP.800-30r1

Joint Task Force, *Risk Management Framework for Information Systems and Organizations: A Security Life Cycle Approach for Security and Privacy*, NIST Special Publication (SP) 800-37 Revision 2, National Institute of Standards and Technology, December 2018, Gaithersburg, Maryland. https://doi.org/10.6028/NIST.SP.800-37r2

National Institute of Standards and Technology, *Risk Tolerance*, Computer Security Resource Center: Glossary [Web site]. Available at https://csrc.nist.gov/glossary/term/risk-tolerance

Department of Homeland Security, *AppVet Mobile App Vetting Service* [Web site]. Available at https://sharedservices.dhs.gov/appvet_info/about/

J. R. Maximoff, D. R. Kuhn, M. D. Trela, and R. Kacker, "A method for analyzing system state-space coverage within a t-wise testing framework," *2010 IEEE International Systems Conference*, San Diego, California, April 5-8, 2010, pp. 598-603. https://doi.org/10.1109/SYSTEMS.2010.5482481

G. J. Myers, T. Badgett, T. M. Thomas, and C. Sandler, *The art of software testing*, 3rd ed. Hoboken, New Jersey: John Wiley & Sons, 2012.

H. Chen, T. Zou, and D. Wang, "Data-flow Based Vulnerability Analysis and Java Bytecode," *7th WSEAS International Conference on Applied Computer Science*, Venice, Italy, November 21-23, 2007, pp. 201-207. Available at http://www.wseas.us/e-library/conferences/2007venice/papers/570-602.pdf

University of Maryland, *FindBugs - Find Bugs in Java Programs* [Web site]. Available at http://findbugs.sourceforge.net/

R. Shah, *Vulnerability Assessment of Java Bytecode* [Thesis], Auburn University, December 16, 2005. http://hdl.handle.net/10415/203

2008 The Ninth International Conference on Web-Age Information Management, WAIM 2008. Piscataway, New Jersey: IEEE [Web site]. http://ieeexplore.ieee.org/servlet/opac?punumber=4596966

Department of Defense (DoD), *Mobile Application Security Requirements*, DoD Memorandum, October 6, 2017. Available at https://iasecontent.disa.mil/stigs/pdf/2017-10-06_DoD_CIO_Mobile_Applications_Security_Memo_Signed.pdf

National Institute of Standards and Technology, *NIST Special Publication 800-53*, [Web site]. Available at https://nvd.nist.gov/800-53

H. G. Rice, "Classes of recursively enumerable sets and their decision problems," *Transactions of the American Mathematical Society*, vol. 74, no. 2, pp. 358-366, March 1953. https://doi.org/10.2307/1990888

Microsoft Corporation, *The STRIDE Threat Model* [Web site], November 11, 2009. Available at https://docs.microsoft.com/en-us/previous-versions/commerce-server/ee823878(v%3dcs.20)

National Institute of Standards and Technology, *SAMATE: Tool Survey* [Web site], https://samate.nist.gov/index.php/Tool_Survey.html

G. Howell and M. Ogata, *An Overview of Mobile Application Vetting Services for Public Safety*, NIST IR 8136, National Institute of Standards and Technology, Gaithersburg, Maryland, January 2017. https://doi.org/10.6028/NIST.IR.8136

Committee on National Security Systems, *Committee on National Security Systems (CNSS) Glossary*, CNSSI No. 4009, April 2015. Available at https://rmf.org/wp-content/uploads/2017/10/CNSSI-4009.pdf

National Institute of Standards and Technology, *Security Content Automation Protocol* [Web site]. Available at https://csrc.nist.gov/projects/security-content-automation-protocol

The MITRE Corporation, *CAPEC - Common Attack Pattern Enumeration and Classification* [Web site]. Available at https://capec.mitre.org

National Information Assurance Partnership (NIAP), *Product Compliant List* [Web site]. Available at https://www.niap-ccevs.org/Product/

J. M. Stecklein, J. Dabney, B. Dick, B. Haskins, R. Lovell, and G. Moroney, "Error Cost Escalation Through the Project Life Cycle," *14th Annual International Symposium*, Toulouse, France, 2004. Available at https://ntrs.nasa.gov/search.jsp?R=20100036670

M. Bartock, M. Souppaya, J. Cichonski, M. Smith, G. Witte, and K. Scarfone, *Guide for Cybersecurity Event Recovery*, NIST Special Publication (SP) 800-184, National Institute of Standards and Technology, Gaithersburg, Maryland, December 2016. https://doi.org/10.6028/NIST.SP.800-184

S. Khandelwal, "New Ransomware Not Just Encrypts Your Android But Also Changes PIN Lock," *The Hacker News*, October 13, 2017. Available at https://thehackernews.com/2017/10/android-ransomware-pin.html

W. A. Jansen, T. Winograd, and K. Scarfone, *Guidelines on Active Content and Mobile Code*, NIST Special Publication (SP) 800-28 Version 2, National Institute of Standards and Technology, Gaithersburg, Maryland, March 2008. https://doi.org/10.6028/NIST.SP.800-28ver2

T. Brewster, "When 'Grandma-Proof' Android Spyware Is Good Enough For International Espionage," *Forbes*, May 15, 2018. Available at https://www.forbes.com/sites/thomasbrewster/2018/05/15/apple-iphone-spouseware-used-in-pakistan-government-attacks/#74f2e2515668

S. Dent, "Report finds Android malware pre-installed on hundreds of phones," *Engadget*, May 24, 2018. Available at https://www.engadget.com/2018/05/24/report-finds-android-malware-pre-installed-on-hundreds-of-phones

H. Zhang, D. She, and Z. Qian, "Android Root and its Providers: A Double-Edged Sword," *Proceedings of the 22nd ACM SIGSAC Conference on Computer and Communications Security (CCS '15)*, Denver, Colorado, October 12-16, 2015, pp. 1093–1104. https://doi.org/10.1145/2810103.2813714

J. P. Mello, Jr, "Marcher Malware Poses Triple Threat to Android Users," *Tech News World*, November 7, 2017. Available at https://www.technewsworld.com/story/84936.html

D. Palmer, "Irremovable bank data-stealing Android malware poses as Google Chrome update," *ZDNet*, April 29, 2016. Available at https://www.zdnet.com/article/irremovable-bank-detail-stealing-android-malware-poses-as-google-chrome-update

M. Moon, "Malware downloader infects your PC without a mouse click," *Engadget*, June 11, 2017. Available at https://www.engadget.com/2017/06/11/malware-downloader-infects-your-pc-without-a-mouse-click

L. Spector, "5 common SMS text scams, and how to avoid them," *PC World*, March 1, 2016. Available at https://www.pcworld.com/article/3034696/mobile/5-common-sms-text-scams-and-how-to-avoid-them.html

OWASP, *Man-in-the-middle attack* [Web site]. Available at https://www.owasp.org/index.php/Man-in-the-middle_attack

Federal Information Security Modernization Act of 2014, Pub. L. 113-283, 128 Stat. 3073. https://www.govinfo.gov/app/details/PLAW-113publ283